Happy Skills

for Happy Kids !

Ten bright ideas that help kids feel glad !

Printed by CreateSpace,
An Amazon.com Company
Available from Amazon.com

Dedicated to Mackenzie, Brooklyn, Addison, and Emmalynn.
My life is brighter because of you!

Do you sometimes feel
anxious, mad, or sad?
Then use these ten happy skills
to change your mood to glad!

One tiny mouse
keeps quiet and still.
When she feels anxious,
this helps her be calm and chill.

Now it's your turn
to act like a mouse.
Sit up straight, silent,
and still inside of your house.

Two shining stars announce,
"I am smart, and I am bright."
These words encourage them
through the darkest of nights.

Now, act like a star,
and prepare to spread your light.
Hold your head high and proclaim,
"I am smart and bright."

Three big, deep breaths
spin these pinwheels around.
Breathing like this also helps
kids to feel happy and sound.

Here is an idea
for the next time you feel stressed.
Imagine you are blowing a pinwheel,
and take three, big, deep breaths.

Four yellow lemons
are squeezed especially tight.
They turn into delicious lemonade
that tastes just right.

Now, pretend to make lemonade
with a flavor that is sour.
First, pick some lemons,
then squeeze with all of your power.

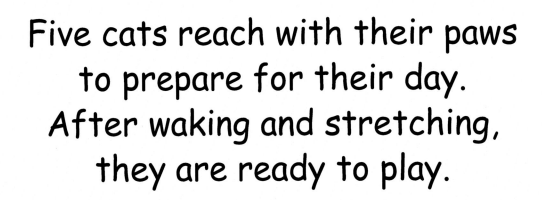

Five cats reach with their paws
to prepare for their day.
After waking and stretching,
they are ready to play.

Now, pretend to be a cat
who is taking life slow.
Slowly raise your arms up,
as high as they will go.

Six green turtles
draw into their shells.
They pull inside tightly
to stay safe and well.

Now, pretend to be a turtle
by pulling your head in tight.
Then, roll your shoulders back
because everything is all right.

Seven lively monkeys
swing from tree to tree.
They smile as they proclaim,
"It's great to be me."

Now, pretend to be a monkey
who is as confident as can be.
Hold your head high and declare,
"It is great to be me!"

Eight tall trees
gently sway in the wind.
They rock back and forth slowly,
stretching with each bend.

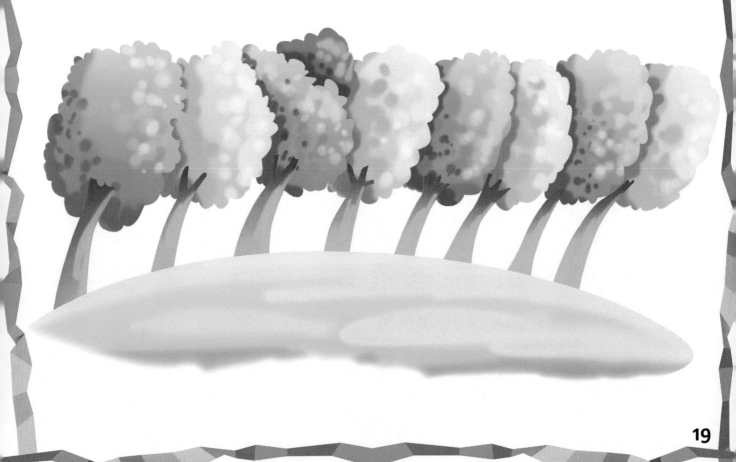

Now, be tall like a tree
while leaning from side to side.
Take your time, stretch slowly,
and enjoy this gentle glide.

Nine happy kids
smile as they play.
Their glad looks declare
it is a marvelous day!

Now, put on a bright smile
that extends from ear to ear.
Let your happy face drive out
all doubt, shame, and fear.

Ten happy hands
wave briskly in the air.
They cheer on family and friends
to show how much they care!

Last but not least, use your hands to give an enormous high five. Connecting with others is important because it will help you to thrive.

But wait! Don't go just yet.
There is one more thing to say.
Be sure to practice these
happiness skills every single day.

The next time you feel
anxious, sad, or mad
put these skills into action,
and change your mood to glad.

Happy Skills For Happy Kids

1. Sit silent and still.
2. Say, "I am smart and bright!"
3. Take three big, deep breaths.
4. Squeeze your hands tight.
5. Stretch your arms high.

6. Roll your shoulders.
7. Say, "It is great to be me!"
8. Stretch from side to side.
9. Smile big.
10. High five a friend.

How Do You Feel?

Happy

Hopeful

Excited

Mad

Scared

Frustrated

Sad

Disappointed

Worried

28

Conversations for Adults and Kids

Make a sad face, and share a time when you felt sad.

Put on your biggest smile. What are three things that make you feel happy?

What is something you are excited about?

What does your mad face look like? What makes you feel mad?

Helping Kids Cope

These ten happiness skills are also called coping skills. A coping skill is any healthy activity that encourages children to relax and reregulate. Of course, adults use coping skills too. These tools help us to manage stress at work, home, and throughout the day. Ideally, coping skills are learned in childhood and continue to develop throughout life.

This section is especially for adults who long to build into the lives of kids. This includes parents, grandparents, foster parents, teachers, and coaches. In addition to containing relevant information about coping skills, there are also ideas for helping kids to get the most out of the strategies in this book. When teaching your kids to manage stress in positive ways, here are three key concepts to keep in mind.

1. Teach through play. Play is how children learn best. The more fun the two of you have when you practice, the more likely your child is to integrate these skills into daily life. So remember to smile, laugh, and cheer your child on as you learn!

2. Form healthy habits by practicing often. The most difficult time for children to use coping skills is when they are upset. So be sure to practice during moments of calm first. Doing this will reduce stress-buildup, and it helps children to form new, healthy habits. Over time, these skills will become so firmly ingrained that your child will apply them naturally!

3. Help kids refine each skill to fit with their unique style. Fortunately, these skills do not need to be practiced in a precise manner. Instead, children should implement them in ways that fit with their unique personalities. So experiment often! The next page provides some additional refinement ideas.

Although there is no single, right way to apply these coping skills, here are some ideas for making them even more effective.

1. **Sit silently and still:** Psychology teaches that our kid's body posture influences how they think and feel. Sitting calmly helps children to feel calm. Practicing this skill is an excellent way to help children to increase their tolerance for being still.

2. **Proclaim, "I am smart and bright!"** Simple self-talk phrases like this one are known as cognitive coping skills. Adults can reinforce cognitive skills throughout the day by repeating the phrases during opportune moments. For example, you might say to your child, "Great job figuring that out. You are smart and bright!" The goal of this particular phrase is to promote your child's self-confidence and independence.

3. **Take three big, deep breaths:** Taking big, deep breaths is so powerful it is taught to adults in anger management courses. Nevertheless, it is so simple that even a two-year-old can use it effectively. Deep breathing helps kids to calm their bodies and quiet their minds. It is also one of the most powerful coping skills around.

4. **Squeeze your hands tight:** This skill is a part of progressive muscle relaxation. Progressive muscle relation involves tensing and relaxing various muscles groups in the body. The goal is to help children to relieve stress while assisting them in recognizing how their body feels differently when it is tense and when it is relaxed. This particular skill is perfect for classroom circle time and during difficult conversations, with one simple twist. Have your child fold his hands together in his lap. Squeeze both hands firmly together. Then, relax both hands while continuing to maintaining eye contact. This allows your child to use a coping skill while also paying attention to you or to the classroom teacher.

5. **Stretch your arms up high:** Physical activity is another excellent way that kids can regulate. This coping skill gets children stretching and moving.

6. **Roll your shoulders:** Like adults, kids carry tension in their shoulders and neck. Children can tense and relax their shoulders as a part of progressive muscle relation, or do gentle shoulder roles. Both are excellent ways to relieve stress.

7. **Proclaim, "It's good to be me!"** This is another cognitive coping skill that children can practice throughout the day. Adults can also help kids to make a list of reasons why it is good to be them. This list might include your child's strengths, important people in his or her life, and enjoyable activities.

8. **Stretch from side to side:** Side bends is another simple stretching exercise that helps kids to relax their bodies and relieve stress through movement.

9. **Smile big:** According to psychology, people are biopsychosocial beings. This complex term describes how one's physical body (biology), one's psychology (thoughts and feelings), and one's social connections (relationships with friends and family) all intertwine. Smiling is a biological act that elevates our psychological mood. In other words, when a child acts happy, their body responds by thinking and feeling happier.

10. **High five a friend:** This simple coping skill taps into the power of social connections. Scientists have recently discovered mirror neurons. These powerful cells in the human brain transmit impulses that cause us to mimic the feelings of others. When a child high fives a friend and sees that friend smile, thanks to mirror neurons, he or she will feel happier too.

11. **Stack these skills together:** By far, the best way to use coping skills is to stack them together. One example is to encourage your child to take three big, deep breaths, proclaim, "I am smart and bright," and then give you a big high five. Although each skill can be used independently, when it comes to coping skills, the more your child stacks together, the merrier life will feel!

More Books By Jed

 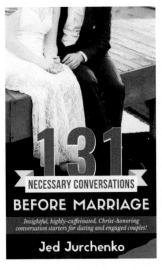  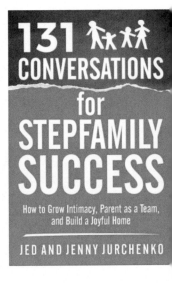

 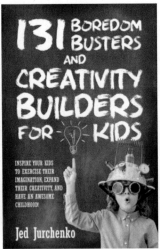  

Find these, and other great titles by Jed, at:
www.coffeeshopconversations.com/books

Made in the USA
San Bernardino, CA
23 July 2018